ISBN 978-0-260-50825-6
PIBN 10952808

CONFERRING OF DEGREES

AT THE CLOSE OF THE SEVENTY-NINTH ACADEMIC YEAR

JUNE 14, 1955

KEYSER QUADRANGLE

AT TEN A. M.

CHIEF MARSHAL

HENRY T. ROWELL

Divisions	Marshals
The President of the University, the Chaplain, Honored Guests, the Trustees	HOWARD E. COOPER
The Faculties	WILLIAM D. McELROY
The Graduates	JOHN WALTON
	WALTER C. BOYER
	WALTER S. KOSKI
	GEORGE S. BENTON
	ROBERT S. AYRE
	JAMES M. McKELVEY
	HSUAN YEH
	GUY L. BRYAN
	JOHN M. STEPHENS
	MARGARET MERRELL
	R. CARMICHAEL TILGHMAN
	WILLIAM C. JOHNSTONE
	RICHARD H. HOWLAND

USHERS

The ushers are members of Kappa Mu Chapter of Alpha Phi Omega
national service fraternity

ORGANIST

JOHN H. ELTERMANN

The audience is requested to stand as the academic procession moves into the area
and to remain standing until after the Invocation and the
singing of the National Anthem

ORDER OF EXERCISES

I
PROCESSIONAL
"Marche Pontificale" by de la Tombelle

II
INVOCATION
RIGHT REVEREND MONSIGNOR JOHN J. DUGGAN
SS. Philip and James Church

III
THE NATIONAL ANTHEM

IV
ADDRESS
DAG HAMMARSKJOLD
Secretary-General of the United Nations

V
CONFERRING OF HONORARY DEGREES

FRANK WHITTEMORE ABRAMS	— presented by Professor PAINTER
HTIN AUNG	— presented by Dean THAYER
DAG HAMMARSKJOLD	— presented by Professor SWISHER

VI
CONFERRING OF DEGREES

Bachelors of Arts	— presented by Dean COX
Bachelors of Engineering Bachelors of Engineering Science Masters of Science in Engineering Doctors of Engineering	— presented by Dean ROY
Bachelors of Science in Business	— presented by Dean ROY
Bachelors of Science Bachelors of Science in Engineering Bachelors of Science in Nursing Masters of Education	— presented by Dean MUMMA
Masters of Science in Hygiene Doctors of Science in Hygiene Masters of Public Health Doctors of Public Health	— presented by Professor HUME
Doctors of Medicine	— presented by Dean BARD
Masters of Arts, School of Advanced International Studies	— presented by Dean THAYER
Masters of Arts Doctors of Philosophy	— presented by Professor PAINTER

VII
BENEDICTION

VIII
RECESSIONAL
"Grand Chorus" by Guilmant

The audience is requested to remain standing after the Benediction
until the faculties have left the area.

CANDIDATES FOR DEGREES

BACHELORS OF ARTS

* WILLIAM HENRY ADAMS, JR., of Glen Burnie, Md.
* LESLIE ALLAN BARD, of Baltimore, Md.
  RICHARD GEORGE BARDES, of Baltimore, Md.
  MYRON BARLOW, of Detroit, Mich.
* HERBERT MAXWELL BARNES, of Roselle Park, N. J.
  CHARLES LEE BARROLL, of Stevenson, Md.
  EDWARD BEHRMAN, of Highland Park, N. J.
  EDMUNDO JOSÉ BERNHEIM, of Managua, Nicaragua
  CARVILLE GODFREY BEVANS, JR., of Baltimore, Md.
  BURTON HOWARD BLOOM, of Baltimore, Md.
* JAY MELVIN BLUMENTHAL, of Baltimore, Md.
  C. ADAM BOCK, JR., of Baltimore, Md.
  PETER JOSEPH BOEHMER, of Douglaston, N. Y.
  MARCEL VIERKE BOELITZ, of New York, N. Y.
  JOSEPH YANCEY BRATTAN, of Baltimore, Md.
  DAVID BROOK, of Brooklyn, N. Y.
* CHARLES PAUL CARLSON, JR., of St. Paul, Minn.
  CHARLES MACKINNON CARLSSON, of Ridgewood, N. J.
  ARTHUR CHARLES CHAUFAUREAUX, of Glendale, Calif.
  GORDON D. CHEEVER, of Baltimore, Md.
  JOHN WELLINGTON CHOATE, of Belmar, N. J.
* DAVID RODMAN COHAN, of Baltimore, Md.
* MAIMON MOSES COHEN, of Baltimore, Md.
  RICHARD COHN, of Monticello, N. Y.
  ROBERT ALLAN COOPER, of Baltimore, Md.
  JOHN PETER CORONEOS, of Baltimore, Md.
* JOSEPH STROTHER CRANE, of Baltimore, Md.
  BENJAMIN FRANKLIN CROUSE, JR., of Baltimore, Md.
  BARRY LEE DAHNE, of Baltimore, Md.
  CARL ANTHONY D'ANGELO, of New York, N. Y.
  WILBUR JOEL DANTZIC, of Baltimore, Md.
  DAVID EDMUND DAVIS, of Baltimore, Md.
  JOHN ALEXANDER DAVIS, of Towson, Md.
* ENRICO FRANK DeMAIO, of New York, N. Y.
  ROBERT ANTHONY DENBY, of Luzerne, Pa.
  MARK EISENBERG, of Baltimore, Md.
  HAROLD AUGUST ENGELKE, JR., of Uniondale, N. Y.
  ROLFE JACK EVENSON, of Verona, N. J.
  CLARENCE EUGENE FAULK III, of Ruston, La.
* GERALD M. FENICHEL, of New York, N. Y.
  JOSEPH NICHOLAS FORBES, of Aquasco, Md.
  TYLER IRA FREEMAN, of New York, N. Y.
* JEFFERSON DAVIS FUTCH III, of Baltimore, Md.

ROBERT CLAIR GABLER, of Baltimore, Md.
* EUGENE HOWARD GALEN, of Perth Amboy, N. J.
* JOHN SCOTT GALLAGHER, of Canton, Ohio
* NORMAN LEO GAMSE, of Miami, Fla.
  HENRY EDWARD GEBHARDT, of Baltimore, Md.
* THOMAS LEWIS GIBSON, JR., of Cumberland, Md.
° JOSEPH WALTER GLUHMAN, of Barberton, Ohio
  IVAN KENNETH GOLDBERG, of Brooklyn, N. Y.
  ALAN MEAD GORDON, of New York, N. Y.
  GEORGE JOSEPH GOUBEAUD, of Jacksonville, Fla.
  FREDERICK NUMA GRIFFITH, of Baltimore, Md.
  PAUL JOHN GROSSCUP, of Baltimore, Md.
  WARREN EDWARD GRUPE, of Drexel Hill, Pa.
  IAN MILTON GUTMAN, of Bradford, Pa.
  EDWARD TOWNSEND HABERMANN, of Hillside, N. J.
  JAMES HERRICK HALL, JR., of Washington, D. C.
  ARTHUR WALDO HAMBLETON, of Baltimore, Md.
* LEROY HANDWERGER, of Baltimore, Md.
  ROBERT MILLER HARRIS, of Lewisburg, W. Va.
  ALBERT LOUIS HARRISON, of Baltimore, Md.
* I. MICHAEL HECHT, of Baltimore, Md.
  CHARLES EDWARD HELMSTETTER, JR., of Jensen Beach, Fla.
  JOHN ARTHUR HENDERSON III, of Wernersville, Pa.
  DAVID ALLEN HILES, of Allison Park, Pa.
* NORMAN HIMELFARB, of Baltimore, Md.
* IRA HOROWITZ, of New York, N. Y.
  EDWARD JOSEPH HYLAND, of Douglaston, N. Y.
* MICHAEL JAWORSKYJ, of Baltimore, Md.
  JONATHAN JENNESS, of Baltimore, Md.
  EDGAR AUGUSTUS JEROME JOHNSON, JR., of Washington, D. C.
  EUGENE EDMUND JOYCE, of Monticello, New York
  ARTHUR BERNARD KALNIT, of Brooklyn, N. Y.
  ALLEN BENJAMIN KAPLAN, of Washington, D. C.
  JAMES THOMAS KEIM, of Baltimore, Md.
  MARVIN MANES KIRSH, of Baltimore, Md.
* JAMES ROBERT KLINENBERG, of Silver Spring, Md.
* DAVID KOTELCHUCK, of Baltimore, Md.
  HANS HEINZ KRIMM, of Kullamaa, Estonia
° JAMES LOUIS KUETHE, JR., of Baltimore, Md.
  MARTIN KUSHNER, of New York, N. Y.
  YAN-LEUNG CAMILLUS KWOK, of Hong Kong, S. China

* Graduating with departmental honors.

Donald William Kydon, of Paterson, N. J.
* James Morrison Lambert, of Baltimore, Md.
Robert V. Lambert, of Baltimore, Md.
James Douglas Laurance, of Towson, Md.
Bernard Lerner, of Baltimore, Md.
Frank S. Levin, of Baltimore, Md.
* Frank Benson Lipps, of Baltimore, Md.
Richard Eugene Lovell, of Baltimore, Md.
Dene Lonier Lusby, of Baltimore, Md.
* Victor Jack Marder, of Baltimore, Md.
Paul Edward McAdam, of Baltimore, Md.
Bruce Probert McLean, of Salisbury, Md.
* Raoul Fink Middleman, of Baltimore, Md.
Jerald Miller, of Perth Amboy, N. J.
Kenneth Maynard Miller, of Chicago, Ill.
Morton Maimon Mower, of Baltimore, Md.
Frank Henry Musial, of Buffalo, N. Y.
Ralph Donald Natale, of Towson, Md.
Maurice John Nelligan, Jr., of Baltimore, Md.
Frederick Palmieri, Jr., of Orange, N. J.
John Joseph Pecora, of Belleville, N. J.
Pascal Anthony Pironti, of Newark, N. J.
William Gable Poist, of Laurel, Md.
Richard Maurice Porterfield, of Hampstead, Md.
Russell LaMonte Poucher, of Yonkers, N. Y.
James Henry Riley, of Baltimore, Md.
Jerry Allan Rose, of Gloversville, N. Y.
Louis Joseph Ruland, Jr., of Baltimore, Md.
Carol Edmund Rybczynski, of Baltimore, Md.
Ramon Santamaria, Jr., of Baltimore, Md.

Daniel Saul Sax, of Baltimore, Md.
Michael William Schindler, of Baltimore, Md.
Duane Philip Schultz, of Baltimore, Md.
* Nelson Bernard Seidman, of Baltimore, Md.
James Wade Shufelt, of Baltimore, Md.
* William Stanley Simon, of Baltimore, Md.
Charles M. Smith, Jr., of Baltimore, Md.
Frederic Matthews Smith, of East Orange, N. J.
Simon Arnold Smith, of Baltimore, Md.
Joseph Arnold Spinzia, of Woodmere, N. Y.
William Alexander Sponsler IV, of Harrisburg, Pa.
* Daniel Jeremy Steinberg, of Washington, D. C.
George Richard Stevens, of Baltimore, Md.
William Sands Stocksdale, of Baltimore, Md.
William Herbert Strutton IV, of Orangeburg, N. Y.
* Jack Sugar, of Baltimore, Md.
* Stephen Siu-Kay Tai, of Baltimore, Md.
Robert Walker Taylor, of Baltimore, Md.
Michael Stephen Tenner, of Baltimore, Md.
Craig Snover Thompson, of Erwinna, Pa.
Paul Martin Tocci, of New York, N. Y.
Jack Terry VanderVen, of Clawson, Mich.
Joseph Frederick Veverka, of Des Moines, Iowa
Albert Saul Weinstein, of New York, N. Y.
Morris Benjamin Wexler, of Baltimore, Md.
Herbert Benjamin Williams, of Lutherville, Md.
Henry Wittich III, of Baltimore, Md.
* Raymond Burger Wuerker, of Baltimore, Md.
* Joseph Abraham Zysman, of New York, N. Y.

(143)

GRADUATING WITH GENERAL HONORS

William Henry Adams, Jr.
Leslie Allan Bard
Jay Melvin Blumenthal
John Wellington Choate
Jefferson Davis Futch, III
Eugene Howard Galen
John Scott Gallagher
Norman Leo Gamse
Thomas Lewis Gibson, Jr.
Leroy Handwerger
I. Michael Hecht
Ira Horowitz

Jonathan Jenness
James Robert Klinenberg
David Kotelchuck
Frank Benson Lipps
Victor Jack Marder
Nelson Bernard Seidman
William Stanley Simon
Daniel Jeremy Steinberg
Jack Sugar
Stephen Siu-Kay Tai
Raymond Burger Wuerker
Joseph Abraham Zysman

* Graduating with departmental honors.

BACHELORS OF ENGINEERING

WILLIAM PENNELL ANDERSON, JR., of Oxford, Md.
WILBERT EDWARD ARMSTEAD, JR., of Baltimore, Md.
BYRON LEE BAIR, of Baltimore, Md.
GEORGE EDWARD BARTOW, of Baltimore, Md.
FREDERICK STUCKY BILLIG, of Bethesda, Md.
FREDERICK RICHARD BLACKBURN, of Hagerstown, Md.
FRANKLIN RICHARD BOWER, of Baltimore, Md.
RONALD GAYLE BRUNN, of Baltimore, Md.
ELMER DONALD CORDES, of Baltimore, Md.
DONALD EARLE COURTS, of Baltimore, Md.
GEORGE CAMERON CREEL, of Darlington, Md.
RONALD MILES CULLISON, of Baltimore, Md.
JOHN PHILIP DEFANDORF, of Milwaukee, Wis.
JAMES EDWARD DENNY, of Baltimore, Md.
CHARLES HENRY FREDERICK, of Baltimore, Md.
STEWART WESLEY GAHAGAN, of Darlington, Md.
WILLIAM RUSSELL GALYON, JR., of Baltimore, Md.
EDWARD SHELDON GOLDBERG, of Baltimore, Md.
HERBERT CHRISTIAN GRIEB, of Baltimore, Md.
DAVID LOUIS HACK, of Nutley, N. J.
JOHN CHARLES HAHN, of Baltimore, Md.
EDMUND FREDERICK HAILE, of Towson, Md.
ROBERT EDWARD HALL, of Baltimore, Md.
GEORGE BROOKE HALLMAN, of Baltimore, Md.
PETER TOBEY HEYL, of New Rochelle, N. Y.
WILLIAM HOWARD HOOVER, JR., of Baltimore, Md.
DONALD WILLIAM HORGAN, of Baltimore, Md.
RICHARD ARLEN HOWELL, of Dundalk, Md.
ALEXANDER FREDERICK JENKINS, JR., of Baltimore, Md.
CHARLES EDWIN JOHNSON, of Crisfield, Md.
ELMER CHARLES JUBB, JR., of Falmouth, Va.
MILLARD DAWSON KEFAUVER, JR., of Keedysville, Md.
BARRETT ENGLE KIDNER, of Baltimore, Md.
JACOB JOHN KRAUSS, of Cresskill, N. J.

JOHN PHILIP LAMBERT, III, of Baltimore, Md.
A. MARIO LOIEDERMAN, of Baltimore, Md.
ANTHONY FRANK MAGGIO, of Baltimore, Md.
LAWRENCE MICHAEL MASTRACCI, of Baltimore, Md.
JOHN JOSEPH McDONOUGH, of Baltimore, Md.
HARRY SAUERS MICKEY, JR., of Baltimore, Md.
WAYNE HAMPTON MILLER, JR., of Baltimore, Md.
SAM MOREKAS, of Baltimore, Md.
ROBERT EUGENE MURPHY, of Baltimore, Md.
FRED ELIOT NATHANSON, of Baltimore, Md.
HARRY EVANS NICHOLSON, of Brunswick, Md.
E. RICHARD NINGARD, of Baltimore, Md.
WILLIAM AUD O'BERRY, of Glen Burnie, Md.
ROBERT MOULTON PACKARD, of Baltimore, Md.
CHARLES OSIRIS PEINADO, of El Paso, Tex.
KENNETH EDWARD PELTZER, of Hampstead, Md.
ROBERT LEE POTTER, of Hagerstown, Md.
CHARLES LUTHER POWELL, of Woodsboro, Md.
CHARLES EUGENE QUIGLEY, of Chevy Chase, Md.
LAWRENCE LEONARD ROUCH, JR., of Baltimore, Md.
CHARLES ALBERT RUTKOWSKI, of Baltimore, Md.
ALLEN ISAAC SINSKY, of Baltimore, Md.
ROBERT EIRY SMITH, of Federalsburg, Md.
WILLIAM KEVIN SMITH, of Baltimore, Md.
GEORGE RUSSELL SPRINGHAM, JR., of Baltimore, Md.
FREDERICK PHILIP STORM, JR., of Baltimore, Md.
CHARLES LEE STOVER, of Baltimore, Md.
JAMES JOSEPH THROWER, JR., of Baltimore, Md.
FREDERICK CRAWFORD VOGT, of Havre de Grace, Md.
RUDOLPH CARL WALCH, JR., of Frederick, Md.
DAVID WENTZ, of Brandywine, Md.
JOHN ROBERT WOTELL, of Baltimore, Md.
JOHN RAYMOND YAKUBISIN, of Elizabeth, N. J.
ERNST HOWARD YOUNG, JR., of Baltimore, Md.

(68)

GRADUATING WITH HONORS

WILLIAM PENNELL ANDERSON, JR.
JACOB JOHN KRAUSS
CHARLES OSIRIS PEINADO

ALLEN ISAAC SINSKY
RUDOLPH CARL WALCH, JR.
ERNST HOWARD YOUNG, JR.

BACHELORS OF ENGINEERING SCIENCE

ALI ARMAN, of Istanbul, Turkey
RONALD WILLIAM ARMSTRONG, of Baltimore, Md.
JORGE BERNHARD BESSIN, of Caracas, Venezuela
LAWRENCE E. BIEMILLER, JR., of Baltimore, Md.
HENRY RUDOLPH BOHNENBERG, JR., of Baltimore, Md.
NEPTALI ANDRADE BONIFAZ, of Quito, Ecuador
WALLACE MEZICK BOUNDS, of Salisbury, Md.

THOMAS RICHARD BRADLEY, of Baltimore, Md.
THOMAS STRATTON BUSTARD, of Baltimore, Md.
LOUIS JOSEPH COLEMAN, of Baltimore, Md.
TILFORD CAMERON CREEL, of Darlington, Md.
GRIFFITH HOLLISTER DAVIS, of Baltimore, Md.
GORDON LUTHER FILBEY, JR., of Baltimore, Md.
JOHN RANDALL GRIFFITH, of Wilmington, Del.

WILLIAM STEPHENSON HARE, of Waldorf, Md.
DONALD FRANCIS HASKELL, of Baltimore, Md.
DENNIS FRANCIS HASSON, of Baltimore, Md.
FRANCIS MILTON HECK, JR., of Hagerstown, Md.
JOSEPH ANTON HEINRICHS, of Baltimore, Md.
ARTHUR SLAYMAKER HERMAN, JR., of Baltimore, Md.
JOHN IRVIN HUDGINS, of Baltimore, Md.
JAN KREBS, of Still Pond, Md.
RUDOLF GERHARD KUSTER, of Baltimore, Md.
ROBERT WILLIAM LANG, of Medford, Mass.
IGOR LELIAKOV, of Baltimore, Md.
FRANK PIERCE LINAWEAVER, JR., of Baltimore, Md.
FORREST EUGENE LOGAN, of Baltimore, Md.

JAMES HOLM LOVE, of Baltimore, Md.
HARRY HERMAN MOTTEK, of Baltimore, Md.
DONALD JAMES PETERSEN, of Towson, Md.
JEROME EMIL RUZICKA, of Baltimore, Md.
DONALD JAY SASS, of Baltimore, Md.
EDWARD FRANCIS SHOCKEY, of Baltimore, Md.
MAURICE SASSON SOUSSA, of Baghdad, Iraq
HARRY EDWIN SPARHAWK, JR., of Owings Mills, Md.
EDMUND THEOPHIL URBANSKI, of Baltimore, Md.
DONALD RICHARD WEBBER, of Westfield, N. J.
ALLAN WHATLEY, JR., of Cambridge, Md.
DONALD ARTHUR WILLIAMS, of Baltimore, Md.
MORTON LEE WOLPERT, of Baltimore, Md.

(40)

GRADUATING WITH HONORS

ARTHUR SLAYMAKER HERMAN, JR.   JEROME EMIL RUZICKA
                        EDMUND THEOPHIL URBANSKI

MASTERS OF SCIENCE IN ENGINEERING

WITH TITLES OF ESSAYS

WINSTON DOUGLAS BABER, of Hampton, Va., B. S. Virginia Military Institute, 1951. Sanitary Engineering.

A Comparison of Single and Two Stage Chlorination of a Sewage Effluent.

PAUL DEWEY BELZ, of Glen Burnie, Md., B. S. Virginia Polytechnic Institute, 1943. Mechanical Engineering.

Vibrations of a Single Degree of Freedom System Having a Time Variable Spring Characteristic.

JAMES MITCHELL BOWER, of Bedford, Va., B. S. Virginia Military Institute, 1950. Sanitary Engineering.

The Removal of a Textile Fiber From a Wool Washing Waste.

WILLIAM MILTON BROWN, of Baltimore, Md., B. S. West Virginia University, 1952. Electric Engineering.

Noise Statistics after Transformations Commonly Found in Circuits.

EDWARD DORSEY BURGER, of Frederick, Md., B. E. The Johns Hopkins University, 1951. Civil Engineering.

The Determination of the Static and the Dynamic Moduli of Elasticity for Wire and Cable.

LYNN RICHARD CHANNELL, of Huttonsville, W. Va., B. S. West Virginia Wesleyan College, 1947; B. S. West Virginia University, 1950. Sanitary Engineering.

The Investigation of a Possible Single-Stage Medium for Use with the Membrane Filter in Coliform Determinations.

JOHN CHARLES COLLINS, of London, England, B. S. University College London, 1952. Sanitary Engineering.

The Inhibition of a Slime Staining Synthetic Fibres in the Viscose Process.

NIRMAL SINGH DHILLON, of New Delhi, India, B. S. East Punjab University, 1950. Sanitary Engineering.

Decomposition of Guanidine and Related Nitrogenous Material in Chemical Manufacturing Wastes.

RALPH LYNDE DISNEY, of Baltimore, Md., B. E. The Johns Hopkins University, 1952. Industrial Engineering.

Analysis of Delivery Dates and Temporary Storage in a Jobbing Shop.

RUBIN FELDMAN, of St. Louis, Mo., B. S. Ch. E. Washington University, 1952. Chemical Engineering.

Inter- and Intra-Phase Transfer Rates from a Volatile Solid into a Turbulent Air Stream.

LEONARD LEE FRANCE, of Baltimore, Md., B. E. The Johns Hopkins University, 1953. Mechanical Engineering.

The Effect of a Grain Boundary on the Mechanical Properties of Aluminum Bicrystals of Controlled Orientation.

ALLEN FRANCIS GATES, of Towson, Md., B. E. The Johns Hopkins University, 1950. Electrical Engineering.

The Design of an Inexpensive Temperature Controller.

EDMUND GILL HART, of Baltimore, Md., B. E. The Johns Hopkins University, 1953. Civil Engineering.

An Analysis for Partially Penetrating Sand Drains.

JOACHIM KUMPF, of Bonn-Lengsdorf, Germany, Dipl. Ing. Institute of Technology, Stuttgart, 1954. Sanitary Engineering.

Surface Tension and Rate of Oxygen Transfer of a Detergent Solution.

LEE SMITH MAGNESS, of Joppa, Md., B. E. The Johns Hopkins University, 1950. Mechanical Engineering.

Residual Stress in Seam Welded Tubing.

SHIRLEY NICKERSON MILLS, JR., of Baltimore, Md., B. A. Carleton College, 1950. Mechanical Engineering.

Measurements of Pressures and Impulses Associated with Blast Waves.

BENNO PAULI, of Baltimore, Md., Civil Engineering.

Equivalent Beam Correlation for Influence Lines of Continuous Trusses.

JOSEPH EDWARD PIPKIN, of Baltimore, Md., B. E. The Johns Hopkins University, 1948. Electrical Engineering.

An Extension of the Watson-Watt Technique of Radio Direction Finding.

ALBERT HENRY PLANTHOLT, of Baltimore Md., B. E. The Johns Hopkins University, 1948. Mechanical Engineering.

Observation of Fluid Flow Phenomena by the Tellurium Method.

CHARLES ALBERT POWELL, of Baltimore, Md., B. E. The Johns Hopkins University, 1950. Electrical Engineering.

Application of Microwave Radio in the Power Utility Field.

HOWARD MCCLELLAN PRYOR, of Glen Burnie, Md., Graduate of United States Air Force Institute of Technology, 1950. Industrial Engineering.

Production Graphic Analysis.

WILLIAM HERMAN SCHWARZ, of Baltimore, Md., B. E. The Johns Hopkins University, 1951. Chemical Engineering.

Mass Transfer in a Wetted Wall Column Turbulent Flow.

EDWARD WALTER SOMERS, of Baltimore, Md., B. E. The Johns Hopkins University, 1953. Civil Engineering.

Total Moment and Shear Curves for Continuous Beams with Variable Moment of Inertia.

RAYMOND FREDERICK TENNEY, of Greenfield, Mass., B. S. University of Massachusetts, 1953. Electrical Engineering.

The Potential Analogue.

THOMAS EATON WATSON, of Baltimore, Md., B. E. The Johns Hopkins University, 1950. Electrical Engineering.

A Description and Evaluation of Microstrip and Stripline.

FRANCIS JOHN WITT, of Baltimore, Md., B. E. The Johns Hopkins University, 1953. Electrical Engineering.

Review of Theories of Conduction and Thermionic Emission Mechanisms in Oxide Coated Cathodes.

(26)

DOCTORS OF ENGINEERING

WITH TITLES OF DISSERTATIONS

SALAMON ESKINAZI, of Baltimore, Md., B. S. in M. E. Robert College, Istanbul, 1946; M. S. in M. E. University of Wyoming, 1948. Mechanical Engineering.

An Investigation of Fully Developed Turbulent Flow in a Curved Channel.

CHARLES DENHARD FLAGLE, of Baltimore, Md., B. E. The Johns Hopkins University, 1940, M. S. E. 1954. Industrial Engineering.

Random Demand as a Factor in Allocation of Organizational Resources.

JOHN HENRY HOKE, of Greencastle, Pa., B. S. Pennsylvania State College, 1946, M. S. 1948. Mechanical Engineering.

Structural Alterations Accompanying the Deformation of Molybdenum Single Crystals in Compression.

MICHAEL LAURIENTE, of Chicago, Ill., B. S. in Met. Eng. Michigan College of Mining and Technology, 1943; M. S. in Met. Eng. 1947. Mechanical Engineering.

The Effect of Macroscopic Imperfections on the Strength of Aluminum Single Crystals.

HENRY STANTON MCDONALD, of Baltimore, Md., B. E. E. Catholic University of America, 1950; M. S. E. The Johns Hopkins University, 1953. Electrical Engineering.

Second Order Contactor Servomechanisms.

RUDOLPH XAVER MEYER, of Annapolis, Md., Dipl. Ing. Swiss Institute of Technology, 1945. Mechanical Engineering.

Interference due to Viscous Wakes between Stationary and Rotating Blades in Turbomachines.

ROMAN ANDREW PASKA, of Baltimore, Md., B. E. E. Villanova College, 1947. Electrical Engineering.

VHF Breakdown of Air at Low Pressures.

JULIUS RAY RUETENIK, of Lakewood, Ohio, B. S. University of Florida, 1946; M. S. Case Institute of Technology, 1949. Mechanical Engineering.

The Investigation of Equilibrium Flow in a Slightly Divergent Channel.

ALBERT PHILIP TALBOYS, of Pasadena, Tex., B. S. Cornell University, 1944. Sanitary Engineering.

A Basic Approach to the Radioactive Laundry Waste Problem.

NOBUHISA UJIIYE, of Tokyo, Japan, B. S. University of Tokyo, 1950. Mechanical Engineering.

The Structural Changes in Molybdenum Single Crystals Due to Cold-Rolling.

ERIC WEGER, of Baltimore, Md., B. E. The Johns Hopkins University, 1951; M. S. E. 1953. Chemical Engineering.

Rate Studies in a Tubular Reactor.

(11)

BACHELORS OF SCIENCE IN BUSINESS

JAMES ATVILL CONNER, of Baltimore, Md.
DONALD GRANT, of Baltimore, Md.
RICHARD PERRY LINDSLEY, of Wenham, Mass.
RICHARD HOWARD MOORE, of South Bend, Ind.

STEVEN RICHARD PASSERMAN, of New York, N. Y.
ALAN JAY RUPRECHT, of Batavia, N. Y.
JOHN BROOKE SHEHAN, JR., of Baltimore, Md.
BARTOW VAN NESS, III, of Baltimore, Md.

(8)

BACHELORS OF SCIENCE

E. WINIFRED ALT, of Owings Mills, Md.
MARJORIE LINDELL BAKER, of Baltimore, Md.
STEPHEN BASARAB, of Madera, Pa.
THOMAS LEE BATEMAN, JR., of Baltimore, Md.
LEONARD BERS, of Baltimore, Md.
HELEN MAY BETTON, of Baltimore, Md.
WARREN ARTHUR BIRGE, of Baltimore, Md.
MARX JOSEPH BLOCK, of Baltimore, Md.
EDWIN LEVERING BOND, of Baltimore, Md.
IDA WARD BOWMAN, of Baltimore, Md.
CHARLES LOUIS BROWN, of Baltimore, Md.
RUTH WADE CAFFREY, of Baltimore, Md.
ROBERT LEE CAMPBELL, of Aberdeen, Md.
GLENN BRYAN CARPENTER, of Baltimore, Md.
HOWARD EDWARD CHANEY, of Baltimore, Md.
KATHRYN RUTH CLARK, of Baltimore, Md.
MICHAEL JAMES CLEARY, III, of Memphis, Tenn.
KATHRYN FLANIGAN DEAN, of Baltimore, Md.
JOHN GORDON DUBAY, of Baltimore, Md.
SHIRLEY RAE DUFF, of Washington, D. C.
MARGARET ANNE EVERING, of Baltimore, Md.
GEORGE ROBERT FAUST, of Baltimore, Md.
THOMAS ORLANDO FIGART, of Baltimore, Md.
MARTIN RICHARD FISHER, of Woodlawn Heights, Md.
LOTTIE ROBERTA FISHPAW, of Upperco, Md.
WILLIAM CAMPBELL FRASER, JR., of Baltimore, Md.
JAMES HOMER FRY, of Baltimore, Md.
ANDREW COLIN GILLIS, JR., of Pasadena, Md.

WILLIAM FREDERICK GLISS, JR., of Baltimore, Md.
ROBERT ALEXANDER GOURLAY, of Towson, Md.
LYLE BLAINE GRAY, of Baltimore, Md.
EMILY BERYL HAMILTON HILL, of Baltimore, Md.
BARBARA McCABE HOPKINS, of Baltimore, Md.
WILLIAM GEORGE JOHNSON, of Baltimore, Md.
RUTH KATHRYN HALL JOHNSTON, of Baltimore, Md.
JAY SEYMOUR KATZ, of Baltimore, Md.
JOHN BAILEY KING, JR., of Baltimore, Md.
JANET BROCK KOUDELKA, of Baltimore, Md.
IRENE AMBORN LAWDER, of Baltimore, Md.
ELIZABETH MEITZLER LEBHERZ, of Baltimore, Md.
RHEA SCHLEGEL LECOMPTE, of Baltimore, Md.
RICHARD LINCOLN LEE, of Arbutus, Md.
MABEL IRWIN LEWIS, of Baltimore, Md.
WILLIAM WATHEN LEWIS, of Baltimore, Md.
MARY LUCILLE BRYANT LUPIEN, of Baltimore, Md.
ALVINA McDONALD, of Baltimore, Md.
DAVID EVEREST McGRANAGHAN, of Olean, N. Y.
HUGH GRIMES MONAGHAN, of Baltimore, Md.
CORNELIUS FRANCIS OBERLE, of Baltimore, Md.
PETER DARR PAUL, of Linthicum Heights, Md.
MARVIN PRESSLER REESER, of Baltimore, Md.
ALBERT EDOUARD RENAUD, III, of Baltimore, Md.
WALTER RHEINHEIMER, of Middle River, Md.
PAUL WALTER ROSEMARK, of Sioux City, Iowa
WOLFGANG ROTENBERG, of Baltimore, Md.
PETER SHAPRAS, of Baltimore, Md.

DAVID MCGREGOR SHIPLEY, III, of Westminster, Md.
CRESTON MARTIEN SMITH, JR., of Baltimore, Md.
BETSY POWELL SNYDER, of Baltimore, Md.

JOHN DENNIS STARIN, of Long Island, N. Y.
BETTY WASHINGTON WHITING, of Baltimore, Md.
MARION FREYER WOLFF, of Silver Spring, Md.

(62)

GRADUATING WITH HONORS

E. WINIFRED ALT
THOMAS LEE BATEMAN, JR.
WARREN ARTHUR BIRGE

BARBARA MCCABE HOPKINS
MARVIN PRESSLER REESER
MARION FREYER WOLFF

BACHELORS OF SCIENCE IN ENGINEERING

RICHARD ACKLER, of Baltimore, Md.
IRVIN HENRY BEIGEL, of Baltimore, Md.
SUBODH CHANDRA BHATTACHARJEE, of Howrah, India
WILLIAM KOLL BOETTINGER, of Baltimore, Md.
CHARLES ANTHONY BUTLER, of Edgewood, Md.
HENRY JOSEPH BUTLER, of Severna Park, Md.
WINFRED STANLEY CONKLIN, of Towson, Md.
CHARLES HENRY CRASS, of Baltimore, Md.
WILLIAM FRANK DRAGER, of Catonsville, Md.
SAMUEL GORDON DUKE, of Baltimore, Md.
JOSEPH HENRY FISHER, of Severna Park, Md.
RAY ROSSELOT FORSEILLE, of Baltimore, Md.
LOUIS FRANZ FREITAG, of Baltimore, Md.
OTHO JAMES HAYNIE, JR., of Pikesville, Md.
JOHN HENRY HUDSON, of Baltimore, Md.
PHILIP STANDIFORD JOHNSON, of Baltimore, Md.
GEORGE IRWIN JOHNSTON, of Baltimore, Md.
BEVERLY BROADDUS JONES, of Towson, Md.
ALEXANDER LOUIS KARPINSKI, of Baltimore, Md.
RICHARD ALAN KEHS, of Baltimore, Md.
ARTHUR WALTER KOPICKY, of Baltimore, Md.
JACK EDWARD KRAFT, of Baltimore, Md.
ROBERT HEFFNER LAWRENCE, of Baltimore, Md.
THOMAS ELDRED LYNCH, of Towson, Md.

CHARLES BENJAMIN MCCLURE, JR., of Baltimore, Md.
NORMAN HENRY MCELROY, of Baltimore, Md.
HENRY HERMAN MILLER, of Baltimore, Md.
LISTON WORTHINGTON NICKLES, of Baltimore, Md.
FRED NILSEN, of Baltimore, Md.
MARION EARL OWENS, of Baltimore, Md.
AMERICO EUGENE PIPPI, of Baltimore, Md.
IRVIN SCOTT POEHLMAN, of Towson, Md.
LAWRENCE HENRY REECAMPER, of Baltimore, Md.
SIDNEY ROEDEL, of Baltimore, Md.
ANDREW ABRAHAM RUDA, of York, Pa.
HOWARD JAMES SALE, of Baltimore, Md.
SAMUEL BATEMAN SHOCKLEY, of Baltimore, Md.
CHARLES GORDON SPIELMAN, of Catonsville, Md.
GUSTAVUS OBER THOMAS, of Baltimore, Md.
RICHARD HENRY TIMM, of Baltimore, Md.
JAMES BALDWIN VOGT, of Baltimore, Md.
MILAN WEAVER WALKER, of Baltimore, Md.
FRANK JOSEPH WASOWICZ, of Baltimore, Md.
STANLEY GORDON WEBB, of Severna Park, Md.
RENOUX WELLER, of Baltimore, Md.
LLOYD LINWOOD WELLS, of Baltimore, Md.
FREDERICK LLEWELLYN WENTWORTH, of Baltimore, Md.
ALBERT MERRILL ZAHN, of Baltimore, Md.

(48)

GRADUATING WITH HONORS

WILLIAM FRANK DRAGER
LOUIS FRANZ FREITAG

PHILIP STANDIFORD JOHNSON
BEVERLY BROADDUS JONES

FREDERICK LLEWELLYN WENTWORTH

BACHELORS OF SCIENCE IN NURSING

ANNA JEAN ALTMAN, of Spartanburg, S. C.
LURENA GAYLE BANGHART, of Greenwich, Conn.
LOIS CLAIRE BAXTER, of Sandusky, Ohio
MARGARET ANNE BUCHANAN, of Bethesda, Md.
ANNE BUDLONG, of Kingston, R. I.
ENDREA BRUNNER CARROLL, of Raleigh, N. C.
BARBARA LAWLER DENNY, of Los Altos, Calif.
JOAN DEVILBISS, of Tulsa, Okla.

JOSEPHINE P. DONISH, of McAdoo, Pa.
SACHIKO FUKUHARA, of Los Angeles, Calif.
MARILYN ANN FURNAL, of Washington, D. C.
MARIANNE GRUBE, of Lancaster, Pa.
VIRGINIA FRANCES ROACH HOCHSTEIN, of Silver Spring, Md.
PATSY JEAN HUSTED, of Baltimore, Md.
BERNADINE ANN JOHNSON, of Park Ridge, Ill.
TERU KAMIKAWA, of Seabrook, N. J.

CAROL CATHERINE KEALEY, of Macon, Mo.
H. MARGARET KEMNER, of Norristown, Pa.
HELEN PAXENOS LASORSA, of Baltimore, Md.
CHARLOTTE BURKE LOCKNER, of Alameda, Calif.
ROSE MARY CARMEN MACH, of Baltimore, Md.
NANCY ELIZABETH MALOY, of Pittsburgh, Pa.
JOAN MARTHA MANIAN, of Washington, D. C.
KATHLEEN ANNE MCCORMICK, of Honolulu, Hawaii
SARAH NEWCOMER MORTIMER, of Smithsburg, Md.
MARY ELIZABETH MUMAW, of Baltimore, Md.
JERRY LEAH NEWMAN, of Houston, Tex.
ANN CAROL PARKER, of Silver Spring, Md.
MARY ANN PETERSON, of Santa Fe, N. M.
NANCY ELIZABETH POOL, of Baltimore, Md.
JANICE LENORE POWELL, of Columbus, Ohio
JOANN E. RICE, of Arlington, Va.

SALLY ANN SAMPLE, of St. Albans, Vt.
ALLIE MARIE SANBORN, of Friendsville, Tenn.
LOIS ANNE SEYMOUR, of Syracuse, N. Y.
JEAN LOUISE SHAULIS, of Baltimore, Md.
JEANETTE ELAINE SMITH, of Tallahassee, Fla.
PATRICIA ANNE TILTON, of Los Angeles, Calif.
ANN RAE TIMANUS, of Baltimore, Md.
MARGARET BARBER TREVER, of Pierre, S. D.
NANCY LEE TRUE, of Lake Wales, Fla.
EMILY GOSSLER VONDERSMITH, of Cincinnati, Ohio
MARY ELIZABETH WATSON, of Poteau, Okla.
MYRA KAUKA WATTS, of Honolulu, Hawaii
MARGARET LOUISE WHITAKER, of Springfield, Ohio
FRANCHELLE WILKINSON, of Decatur, Ill.
EMILY KATHERINE WYNN, of Waycross, Ga.

(47)

MASTERS OF EDUCATION

ANN GILLIS BUESCHEL, of Baltimore, Md., A. B. Goucher College, 1949.

JOEL ACUS CARRINGTON, of Baltimore, Md., A. B. Howard University, 1948.

THOMAS ALVORD CARTMILL, of Baltimore, Md., B. S. Springfield College, 1949.

EDWARD LEMOINE CRILL, of Elgin, Ill., A. B. Manchester College, 1946.

ELAINE CARSLEY DAVIS, of Baltimore, Md., B. S. Coppin Teachers College, 1942; B. S. Morgan State College, 1943; LL. B. University of Maryland, 1950.

WESTON LAWRENCE DEAN, of Baltimore County, Md., B. S. University of Maryland, 1948.

WILLIAM KAILER DUNN, of Baltimore, Md., A. B. Catholic University of America, 1934; M. A., 1935.

WILLIAM STANLEY EISNER, of Baltimore, Md., B. S. The Johns Hopkins University, 1946.

ESTELA CASTILLO FELICIANO, of Manila, Republic of the Philippines, B. S. Ed. The Misamis Institute, 1953.

JANE CARTWRIGHT GOUSHA, of Tiffin, Ohio, A. B. Heidelberg College, 1947.

WILLIAM NOELLERT JOHNSTON, of Brooklyn, N. Y., A. B. The Johns Hopkins University, 1949.

HENRY WILLIAM KUEHNLE, JR., of Baltimore, Md. A. B. The Johns Hopkins University, 1950.

WILLIAM GOODFELLOW LAND, of Washington, D. C., A. B. Harvard University, 1928; A. M. 1931.

WILLIAM JOHN MARCK, JR., of Baltimore, Md., A. B. The Johns Hopkins University, 1950.

RUTH JANE TIMANUS MAXWELL, of Lutherville, Md., B. S. The Johns Hopkins University, 1951.

MARIE LOUISE EWING REDCAY, of Reisterstown, Md., B. S. The Johns Hopkins University, 1953.

CALVERT EARL SCHLICK, JR., of Baltimore, Md. A. B. The Johns Hopkins University, 1952.

ELIZABETH SNEAD SHUE, of Baltimore, Md., A. B. Maryville College, 1940.

MILTON EDWARD STANLEY, of Baltimore, Md., B. S. Teachers College Columbia University, 1949.

BERNARD JOHN STINNETT, of Baltimore, Md., A. B. The Johns Hopkins University, 1935.

JOHN ROBERT SUTTON, III, of Baltimore, Md., A. B. Western Maryland College, 1949.

(21)

MASTERS OF SCIENCE IN HYGIENE

WITH TITLES OF THESES

ELEANOR BOWLES ARMISTEAD, of Staunton, Va., A. B. Mary Baldwin College, 1947. Microbiology.

Quantitative Studies of the Wassermann Antibody-Cardiolipin Immune System: Antibody Estimations in Absolute Weight Units.

BETSY MORTON HILL, of Roanoke, Va., A. B. Hollins College, 1936. Microbiology.

Kinetic Studies on Complement Fixation.

LILLIAN E. OLMEDA NIEVES, of Hato Rey, Puerto Rico, B. S. University of Puerto Rico, 1952. Environmental Medicine (Audiology and Speech).

Relationship among Various Threshold and Supra-Threshold Hearing Tests for Normal and Hearing Impaired Persons.

ANN SNIDER SCHLUEDERBERG, of Baltimore, Md., B. S. Ohio State University, 1950. Microbiology.

Characterization of an Inhibitor of Influenza Virus Hemagglutination Isolated from Human and Pork Lungs.

(4)

DOCTORS OF SCIENCE IN HYGIENE

WITH TITLES OF DISSERTATIONS

SAMUEL HYMAN BROOKS, of Annapolis, Md., B. S. University of Maryland, 1949. Biostatistics.

Comparison of Methods for Estimating the Optimal Factor Combination.

KEITH MORRIS COWAN, of Long Beach, Calif., A. B. University of Southern California, 1948; M. S., 1950. Microbiology.

Lysis of Sheep Erythrocytes by a Long-Chain Polymer, Polyethylene Glycol, and Complement.

ALBERT JAMES HALEY, of Durham, N. H., B. S. University of New Hampshire, 1949; M. S., 1950. Parasitology.

Host Specificity of the Rat Nematode, Nippostrongylus muris.

AMY RUTH KEY, of Warren, Ark., B. S. Hendrix College, 1947. Environmental Medicine (Audiology and Speech).

Psychogalvanic Skin Resistance Responses to Auditory Stimuli in Neuropathology.

HERBERT JOSEPH RAPP, of Baltimore, Md., B. A. The Johns Hopkins University, 1948; Sc. M. in Hyg., 1953. Microbiology.

A Mathematical Theory and Analysis of Immune Hemolysis.

LAURENCE B. SENTERFIT, of Sarasota, Fla., B. S. University of Florida, 1949; M. S., 1950. Parasitology.

The Development of Antibodies in Schistosome Infection as Measured by the Miracidial Immobilization Reaction.

WENDELL NICHOLLS STAINSBY, of Danville, Pa., A. B. Bucknell University, 1951. Environmental Medicine.

The Effect of Passive Stretch on Oxygen Consumption of Skeletal Muscle.

ROEBERT LYLE STEARMAN, of Corvallis, Ore., B. S. Oregon State College, 1947; M. S., 1949. Biostatistics.

A Statistical Estimate of Variation Encountered in Studying Dispersion of Radioactive Phosphorus in Embryonated Chicken Eggs.

DONALD W. TWOHY, of Clackamas, Ore., B. S. Oregon State College, 1948; Sc. M., 1951. Parasitology.

Experimental Studies on Migration and Early Growth of Nippostrongylus muris in the Rat.

(9)

MASTERS OF PUBLIC HEALTH

JOHN HENRY ACKERMAN, U. S. Public Health Service, M. D. Marquette University, 1948.

DONALD MARR ALDERSON, U. S. Air Force, B. S. Med. University of Nebraska, 1933; M. D., 1934.

IVAN STAMENITOV ALIO, of Bolivar, Venezuela, M. D. Eberhard-Karls University of Tübingen, 1945.

ROBERT M. ALTMAN, U. S. Army, B. S. in Agri. University of Florida, 1948. M. of Agri., 1949.

MIR AHMAD ALI KHAN ANWAR, of Karachi, Pakistan, B. Sc. Osmania University, 1942; Ph. D. University of Minnesota, 1949.

FAISSAL CHEIKH EL ARD, of Damascus, Syria, M. D. Friedrich Wilhelm University, Berlin, 1943.

HERNAN BAENA ZAPATA, of Bogota, Colombia, M. D. Xavier Pontifical and Catholic University, Bogota, 1949.

GABINO VALERA BALBIN, of Bangued, Abra, Republic of the Philippines, M. D. University of the Philippines, 1934; C. P. H., 1952.

SOOK BANG, of Seoul, Korea, M. D. Severance Union Medical College, Korea, 1944.

ELIZABETH KESSLER BARE, of Westminster, Md., A. B. Wilson College, 1947; M. N. Yale University, 1950.

GERALD D. BARTON, U. S. Public Health Service, B. S. University of Idaho, 1941; M. D. University of Chicago, 1946.

DAVID HENRY BEYER, U. S. Air Force, M. D. University of Maryland, 1948.

JAMES OLIVER BOND, of Arcadia, Fla., A. B. Earlham College, 1948; M. D. University of Chicago, 1950.

JOSÉ MANUEL BORGOÑO, of Santiago, Chile, M. D. University of Chile, 1950.

BAARD BREKKE, of Oslo, Norway, M. D. University of Oslo, 1946.

ARNOLD WILLIAM BROCKMOLE, of Evansville, Ind., A. B. Evansville College, 1940; M. D. St. Louis University, 1943.

YOUN KEUN CHA, of Pusan, Korea, M. D. Severance Union Medical College, Korea, 1942.

CHARLES EDGAR COOK, JR., U. S. Air Force, A. B. Oklahoma City University, 1938; B. S. Med. University of Oklahoma, 1940; M. D., 1942.

AMBHAN DASANEYAVAJA, of Bangkok, Thailand, M. B. University of Medical Sciences, Bangkok, 1950.

JAMES MALCOLM DAVIS, U. S. Air Force, A. B. Indiana University, 1937; M. D., 1941.

RICHARD MONTGOMERY FENNO, U. S. Air Force, B. S. University of Wisconsin, 1941; M. D., 1949.

LOUIS FINK, of Philadelphia, Pa., D. V. M. Alabama Polytechnic Institute, 1937.

HELEN LOIS FISK, of Baltimore, Md., B. S. New York University, 1940.

THOMAS MICHAEL FLOYD, U. S. Navy, B. S. Howard College, 1936; M. S. University of Chicago, 1948.

JUAN C. GÓMEZ NÚÑEZ, of Maracay, Aragua, Venezuela, B. S. C. E. Pennsylvania Military College, 1944.

OSCAR GOULD, of Asuncion, Paraguay, M. D. National University of Paraguay, 1944.

JOHN RANDOLPH HALL, JR., U. S. Army, A. B. Central College, 1935; B. S. Med. University of Nebraska, 1938; M. D. Washington University, 1939; M. S. Pharm. University of Chicago, 1949.

GEORGE LIVINGSTONE HAMILTON, JR., of Hartford, Conn., A. B. Cornell University, 1936; M. D. Tufts College, 1944.

RICHARD L. HAYES, U. S. Public Health Service, B. S. Thiel College, 1938; D. D. S. University of Michigan, 1949.

THURMAN AUGUST LARSON, U. S. Air Force, B. S. Bowdoin College, 1934; M. D. George Washington University, 1940.

JOSEPH DAVID MANGES, U. S. Army, D. V. M. Kansas State College, 1935.

ROMEO MANRIQUE DE LARA, JR., of Tlalpan, Mexico, M. D. National School of Medicine, Mexico, 1951; M. P. H. School of Health and Hygiene, 1952.

WILLIAM JOSEPH MEYER, of Honeoye, N. Y., A. B. Columbia College, 1931; M. D. University of Pennsylvania, 1941.

VICENTE PINTO MUSA, of Rio de Janeiro, Brazil, M. D. University of Brazil, 1936.

HIROSHI OKADA, of Nagoya, Japan, M. D. Nagoya National University, 1937; D. M. Sc., 1941.

FRANCIS THEODORE OLIVER, of Buffalo, N. Y., B. A. University of Buffalo, 1949; M. D., 1953.

JOSEPHINE G. PATERSON, of Freeport, N. Y., R. N., Dip. Lenox Hill Hospital School of Nursing, 1945; B. S. in N. Ed. St. John's University, 1955.

V. S. RAMASWAMI, of Madras, India, M. B. B. S. Andhra University, 1935; B. S. Sc. University of Madras, 1939.

WILLIAM LIVAN ROSS, JR., U. S. Public Health Service, A. B. Catawba College, 1942; Certif. of Med. University of North Carolina, 1943; M. D. Jefferson Medical College, 1945.

ESPERANZA MANALO-SALINDA, of Baguio City, Republic of the Philippines, M. D. University of the Philippines, 1942.

O'DONNALD HERSCHEL SHEPPARD, of Washington, D. C., M. D. Howard University, 1945; B. S., 1949.

WALTER HAINES SMARTT, U. S. Air Force, B. S. Virginia Military Institute, 1944; M. D. University of Virginia, 1948.

EDWARD MILTON SMITH, JR., U. S. Navy, B. S. University of Maryland, 1944; M. D., 1946.

FATHI A. SOLIMAN, of Cairo, Egypt, M. B., B. Ch. Fouad I University, 1940; D. V. D., 1944.

JOSÉ LUIS SOTO-ALARCÓN, of San Juan, Puerto Rico, B. S. University of Puerto Rico, 1949.

ROBERT EUGENE THOMAS, of Baltimore, Md., A. B. University of Southern California, 1941; M. D., 1951.

KOHEI TOYOKAWA, of Tokyo, Japan, M. D. University of Tokyo, 1938; D. M. Sc., 1947.

ROY PICCIO VILLASOR, of Bacolod City, Republic of the Philippines, M. D. University of the Philippines, 1943.

WILLIAM HARRISON WATSON, JR., U. S. Air Force, D. V. M. University of Georgia, 1950.

TING HSIUNG WONG, of Taipei, Taiwan, China, M. D. National Taiwan University, 1943.

AHMED ZAHER ZAGHLOUL, of Cairo, Egypt, M. B., B. Ch. Cairo University, 1944; D. P. H., 1953.

ABDUL ZAHIR, of Kabul, Afghanistan, B. A. Columbia College, 1935; M. D. Columbia University, 1939.

(52)

DOCTORS OF PUBLIC HEALTH

WITH TITLES OF THESES

EDWARD JAMES DEHNÉ, U. S. Army, B. S. University of North Dakota, 1935; M. D. University of Oregon, 1937; M. P. H. The Johns Hopkins University, 1941. Environmental Medicine.

Effect of Environmental Temperature upon Susceptibility to Toxic Industrial Agents.

HILDA KNOBLOCH, of Baltimore, Md., B. A. Barnard College, 1936; M. D. New York University, 1940; M. P. H. The Johns Hopkins University, 1951. Public Health Administration (Maternal and Child Health).

An Evaluation of a Questionnaire on Infant Development.

EDWARD FALSEN KROHN, of Bergen, Norway, M. D. University of Oslo, 1941; M. P. H. The Johns Hopkins University, 1953. Epidemiology.

An Analysis and Interpretation of the Results of a Study of Tuberculin Reactions in School Children of Baltimore.

HILDEGARD ROTHMUND, of Stuttgart, Germany, M. D. University of Heidelberg, 1945; M. P. H. The Johns Hopkins University, 1950. Public Health Administration (Maternal and Child Health).

A Field Study of Retrolental Fibroplasia in Maryland.

(4)

DOCTORS OF MEDICINE

JAMES CRAWFORD ALLEN, of Lubbock, Tex., A. B. Harvard University, 1951.

CHARLES TESCH AMBROSE, of Noblesville, Ind., A. B. Indiana University, 1951.

LORRAINE TOLMAN BISWANGER, of Baltimore, Md., A. B. University of California at Los Angeles, 1951.

LAURENCE HENRY BLACKBURN, JR., of Cleveland, Ohio, A. B. Princeton University, 1951.

LEWIS EDWARD BRAVERMAN, of Quincy, Mass., A. B. Harvard University, 1951.

MICHAEL S. BUCKNER, of Headland, Ala., S. B., University of Alabama, 1951.

DAVID J. BUNNELL, JR., of New York, N. Y., A. B. Kenyon College, 1951.

OLIVER PETTEBONE CAMPBELL, of Colorado Springs, Col., A. B. Colorado College, 1951.

DONALD EDWARD CAREY, of Cleveland Heights, Ohio, A. B. Princeton University, 1951.

JOHN MILLER CARROLL, of Pittsburgh, Pa., A. B. Yale University, 1950.

JERRIE CHERRY, of Baltimore, Md., A. B. University of Virginia, 1951.

HARRY PAUL CLAUSE, JR., of Baltimore, Md., S. B. Wake Forest College, 1951.

FREEMAN WIDENER COPE, of Montrose, N. Y., A. B. Harvard University, 1951.

WILLIAM STEPHEN COPPAGE, JR., of Baltimore, Md., A. B. The Johns Hopkins University, 1951.

NICHOLAS CUNNINGHAM, of Springfield Centre, N. Y., A. B. Harvard University, 1950.

JAMES HALL DEEN, of Starkville, Miss., S. B. Mississippi State College, 1951.

JERRY GENE DODSON, of Terre Haute, Ind., A. B. Indiana State Teachers College, 1950.

ERIC VAN EISNER, of New York, N. Y., A. B. Princeton University, 1951.

HENRY COFFIN EVERETT, of Boston, Mass., A. B. Harvard University, 1951.

GOTTLIEB CHRISTIAN FRIESINGER, of Zanesville, Ohio, S. B. Muskingum College, 1951.

DONALD ALLAN GOODWIN, of La Canada, Calif., A. B. University of California, 1947.

PETER GOURAS, of Brooklyn, N. Y., A. B. The Johns Hopkins University, 1951.

DONALD PAUL HAHN, of Baltimore, Md., A. B. Princeton University, 1951.

GEORGE ARCHER HARKINS, of Danville, Ky., A. B. Princeton University, 1950.

CHESTER Z. HAVERBACK, of Haverhill, Mass., A. B. Syracuse University, 1948; M. S., 1951.

PAUL CHESLEY HODGES, JR., of Chicago, Ill., Ph. B. University of Chicago, 1948; M. S. University of Wisconsin, 1950.

ALAN FREDERICK HOFMANN, of Hyattsville, Md., A. B. The Johns Hopkins University, 1951.

RICHARD BERNARD HORNICK, of Johnstown, Pa., A. B. The Johns Hopkins University, 1951.

BRENDA HEATH JACOBSEN, of Buffalo, N. Y., A. B. Wellesley College, 1951.

JOHN THOMAS JENKINS, of Oakland, Calif., A. B. Stanford University, 1951.

DAVID KAPLAN, of Durham, N. C., A. B. Williams College, 1951.

FREDERIC MARSHAL KENNY, of New York, N. Y., A. B. Princeton University, 1951.

JOHN CORNELIUS KISTLER, of Baltimore, Md., A. B. The Johns Hopkins University, 1951.

EDMUND WILKING KLINE, of Cuba, N. Y., S. B. Franklin and Marshall College, 1951.

WILLIAM FRANK KNOWLES, of North Hollywood, Calif., S. B. University of California at Los Angeles, 1951.

MICHAEL WYNNE LA SALLE, of Kansas City, Mo., A. B. Washington University, 1950; S. B. University of Missouri, 1952.

JAY M. LEVY, of Baltimore, Md., A. B. The Johns Hopkins University, 1951.

JOHN ADELBERT LYDEN, JR., of Natchez, Miss., A. B. Virginia Military Institute, 1951.

OLIVER NORFLEET MASSENGALE, of Evansville, Ind., A. B. Vanderbilt University, 1951.

HAMILTON WITHERSPOON McKAY, JR., of Charlotte, N. C., A. B. Princeton University, 1951.

MARTIN MELTZER, of Atlantic City, N. J., A. B. Princeton University, 1951.

FRANKLIN LOUIS MITCHELL, JR., of Excelsior Springs, Mo., A. B. University of Missouri, 1951; S. B., 1953.

THOMAS FRANCIS MULLADY, III, of Rockville Centre, N. Y., A. B. The Johns Hopkins University, 1951.

GENEVIEVE ELIZABETH MURRAY, of Andover, Mass., A. B. Radcliffe College, 1951.

WIL BORCHERS NELP, of Franklin, Ind., A. B. Franklin College, 1951.

MAE BANWELL NETTLESHIP, of Little Rock, Ark., S. B., University of Arkansas, 1949.

WILLIAM EDWARD NEUBURGER, of Maplewood, N. J., A. B. Princeton University, 1950.

PETER DEAN OLCH, of Los Angeles, Calif., A. B. Pomona College, 1951.

FLOYD ROSWELL PARKS, JR., of Los Angeles, Calif, A. B. Dartmouth College, 1951.

ROBERT GEORGE PEELER, of Lexington, N. C., A. B. Catawba College, 1951.

HENRY A. PETERSEN, JR., of Houston, Tex., A. B. Princeton University, 1951.

LEON MERWIN PROTASS, of New Britain, Conn., A. B. Wesleyan University, 1951.

WILLIAM JOSEPH RAHILL, III, of Harrisburg, Pa., A. B. Princeton University, 1951.

WILLIAM PAUL REAGAN, of Little Rock, Ark., A. B. Yale University, 1951.

JAMES ALEXANDER REID, of Kezar Falls, Me., A. B. Williams College, 1949; S. B. Massachusetts Institute of Technology, 1949.

GEORGE WESLEY SANTOS, of Maywood, Ill., S. B. and S. M. Massachusetts Institute of Technology, 1951.

PAUL EDGAR SHORB, JR., of Washington, D. C., A. B. Williams College, 1951.

MARY BETTY STEVENS, of Granville, N. Y., A. B. Vassar College, 1948.

JAMES PHILLIPS THOMAS, of Baltimore, Md., A. B. University of North Carolina, 1951.

ROBERT CUSHMAN THOMAS, of East Rochester, N. Y., A. B. Dartmouth College, 1952.

SAMUEL PHILLIP TILLMAN, of Statesboro, Ga., A. B. Emory University, 1951.

FERNANDO GIUSEPPE VESCIA, of Italy, A. B. The Johns Hopkins University, 1951.

ROGER LYLE VON HEIMBURG, of Marinette, Wis., A. B. The Johns Hopkins University, 1951.

JOHN HENRY WARVEL, JR., of Indianapolis, Ind., A. B. Harvard University, 1951.

JOHN FRANKLIN WATSON, of East Orange, N. J., A. B. Dartmouth College, 1952.

WILLIAM LOGAN WEBB, JR., of Little Rock, Ark., A. B. Princeton University, 1951.

CLARENCE SCHOCK WELDON, of Mount Joy, Pa., A. B. University of Michigan, 1951.

JAMES THOMAS WHEELER, of Abilene, Tex., S. B. Baylor University, 1951.

KIRKLEY R. WILLIAMS, of Charlottesville, Va., A. B. University of Virginia, 1952.

DAVID ELIAB WOOD, V, of Germantown, Md., A. B. Harvard College, 1952.

CHARLES EDWARD WRIGHT, of Baltimore, Md., A. B. Centre College of Kentucky, 1951.

ROBERT WATKINS YOUNGBLOOD, of Birmingham, Ala., A. B. Howard College, 1951.

PAUL MICHAEL ZAVELL, of Flint, Mich., A. B. The Johns Hopkins University, 1951.

(73)

MASTERS OF ARTS

IN THE SCHOOL OF ADVANCED INTERNATIONAL STUDIES

RICHARD TAFT ANTOUN, of Shrewsbury, Mass., B. A. Williams College, 1953.

DIRK FLOYD BOLLENBACK, of CAMBRIDGE, Mass., B. A. Wesleyan University, 1953.

MARGARET DREYFUS, of New York, N. Y., A. B. Hunter College, 1954.

MYLES LAFAYETTE GREENE, JR., of Washington, D. C., B. A. Yale University, 1950.

SAMUEL CHARLES KEITER, of Oneonta, N. Y., B. A. Carleton College, 1952.

MARY POWER LIGHTLE, of Washington, D. C., B. A. Stanford University, 1938, M. S. New York School of Social Work, 1941.

WINGATE LLOYD, of Haverford, Pa., A. B. Princeton University, 1953.

MAX ADOLF MAKAGIANSAR, of Djakarta, Indonesia.

ERNEST EMERSON MONTGOMERY, of Northford, Conn., B. A. University of North Carolina, 1952.

KAREN BYL PETERSEN, of New York, N. Y., B. A. University of California, 1953.

KHALIDA BESSIE SHOWKER, of Kingsport, Tenn., B. A. Mary Washington College, 1952.

RUTH SORENSEN SINGER, of Lincoln, Nebr. A. B. University of Nebraska, 1952.

THOMAS STREITHORST, JR., of Haworth, N. J., A. B. Princeton University, 1953.

JOSEPH SIMON SZYLIOWICZ, of Denver, Colo., A. B. University of Denver, 1953.

TOINETTE YVONNE TRIBBLE, of Los Angeles, Calif., A. B. Stanford University, 1953.

MARGARET ANNE TYSON, of New York, N. Y., A. B. College of Mt. St. Vincent, 1950.

DONALD ALBERT WEBSTER, of Rochester, N. Y., A. B. Hamilton College, 1953.

RALPH ROMANS WESTFALL, of Brooklyn, N. Y., B. A., Colgate University, 1953.

(18)

MASTERS OF ARTS

WITH TITLES OF ESSAYS

ELIZABETH ANN BARBER, of Miami, Fla., B. A. Florida
State University, 1953. History.
James G. Blain and the Bering Sea Controversy.

GEORGE FLETCHER BASS, of Annapolis, Md., Oriental Seminary.

WILLIAM SKELLEY BURFORD, of Baltimore, Md., B. A.
Amherst College, 1949. Writing.
The Structure of Consciousness in Dostoevsky's *A Raw
Youth.*

OLIVER DALE COLLINS, III, of Wilmington, Del., A. B. Colgate University, 1953. Chemistry.

MAHMOOD ALI DAUD, of Mosul, Iraq. History.
The Iraqi Revolt of 1920.

BERNHARD DEKLAU, of Baltimore, Md., B. A. The Johns
Hopkins University, 1954. Chemistry.

DONALD EDWARD DETTMORE, of Baltimore, Md., B. S. State
Teachers College, Towson, Md., 1952. History.
The Memelland 1933-1939: Nazi Aggression in Minia-
ture.

NATHAN FAST, of New York, N. Y., A. B. City College of
of New York, 1952. Geography.
Agricultural and Agrarian Problems in Alluvial Iraq.

PRISCILLA LYDIA HOFMANN, of Baltimore, Md., B. A.
Goucher College, 1924. Romance Languages.

RICHARD LAMOND IRWIN, of Baltimore, Md., B. E. The
Johns Hopkins University, 1951. Chemistry.

MICHAEL JAWORSKYJ, of Baltimore, Md., B. A. The Johns
Hopkins University, 1954. Political Science.
The Pure Theory of Law and the Soviet Theory of
State and Law.

BARBARA GRACE JOHNSON, of Baltimore, Md., B. A. Welles-
ley College, 1952. Political Science.
The French Attitude toward the European Defense
Community.

FREDERICK ALEXANDER KING, of Glen Rock, N. J., A. B.
Stanford University, 1953. Psychology.

JAMES ROBERT KLINENBERG, of Silver Spring, Md. Biological Sciences.
A Study of Nitrate Reductase in *Achromobacter
fischeri.*

JAMES LOUIS KUETHE, JR., of Baltimore, Md. Biological
Sciences.
Anxiety, Muscle Tension, and Personality as Deter-
miners of Response Variability.

NORMAN LEE KUSHNICK, of Baltimore, Md., B. A. The
Johns Hopkins University, 1952. Business and Industrial
Management.
Financial Statement Adjustment for Price Level
Changes—A Case Study.

RICHARD ALEXANDER LANE, of Baltimore, Md., B. A. The
Johns Hopkins University, 1954. Biological Sciences.
The Interaction of Hairless with Mutants Producing
Extra Venation in the Wing of *Drosophilia melano-
gaster.*

JAMES BURHANS LAWSON, of Albany, N. Y., B. A. New
York State College for Teachers, 1950. German.
Zur Entstehung der ersten zwei Duineser Elegien.

LAURENCE PEREIRA LEITE, of Chevy Chase, Md. Art.

HARRIET RICHARDS LOWRY, of Washington, D. C., A. B.
Vassar College, 1953. Classics.

VICTOR JACK MARDER, of Baltimore, Md. Biological Sciences.
The Effects of Delay of Retention Test upon the Pat-
tern of Errors in the Retroactive Inhibition of Rote
Serial Learning.

HUBERT MILTON MARTIN, JR., of Chattanooga, Tenn., A. B.
University of Chattanooga, 1954. Classics.

RUTH GOLDWATER MASER, of Baltimore, Md. Poltical Science.
Personalized Justice in the Juvenile Court of Baltimore City.

LAWRENCE VINCENT MCDONNELL, of Baltimore, Md., A. B.
St. Paul's College, 1950. Romance Languages.

GEORGE THOMAS MCGREW, of Timonium, Md., B. S. Western
Maryland College, 1951. Chemistry.

ERIKA LOTTE METZGER, of Kew Gardens, N. Y., A. B.
Queens College, 1952. Romance Languages.

STEPHEN MINOT, of Boston, Mass., A. B. Harvard College,
1953. Writing.
A Novel—Part One.

EUGENE MIRABELLI, JR., of Lexington, Mass., A. B. Harvard
College, 1952. Writing.
A Novel—Part One.

MARC LEON NERLOVE, of Chicago, Ill., B. A. University of
Chicago, 1952. Political Economy.
The Predictive Test as a Tool for Research: The De-
mand for Meat in the United States.

FRANK CHAPPELL OGG, JR., of Bowling Green, Ohio, B. A. Bowling Green State University, 1951. Mathematics.

ALICE ADAMS PADGETT, of Arlington, Va., B. S. American University, 1954. Chemistry.

RAYMOND JOSEPH PIPINO, of Baltimore, Md., B. A. The Johns Hopkins University, 1952. Mathematics.

LUCIA POZZI-ESCOT, of Lima, Peru. Chemist, National University of San Marcos, 1945. Chemistry.

BEVERLY JEAN PRANITIS, of Johnson City, N. Y., A. B. New York State College for Teachers, 1953. Romance Languages.

ARNOLD S. PROSTAK, of Baltimore, Md., B. S. College of William and Mary, 1950. Chemistry.

JUDITH MILDRED RICE, of West Newton, Mass., B. A. Wellesley College, 1952. Romance Languages.

GUENTHER CARL RIMBACH, of Baltimore, Md. German.
Wedekind als Moralist und Versuch einer neuen Interpretation des Dramas: *Die Zensur*.

ARIEH ISAAC SACHS, of Tel Aviv, Israel, B. A. The Johns Hopkins University, 1954. Philosophy.

WILSON LUDLOW SCOTT, of Washington, D. C., B. A. Yale University, 1931. History of Science.
Sources of Boerhaave's Medical Lectures on Physics, with Particular Reference to the Significance of these Lectures to Physical Chemistry.

NELSON BERNARD SEIDMAN, of Baltimore, Md. Business and Industrial Management.
Taxability of Stock Dividends—A Legal and Economic Analysis.

LOUIS JULIUS SHUB, of Baltimore, Md. Romance Languages.

BARBARA ELIZABETH SPRENG, of Cleveland, Ohio, A. B. Oberlin College, 1954. Classics.

GEORGE RICHARD STEVENS, of Baltimore, Md., A. B. The Johns Hopkins University, 1954. Geology.

EDWARD JOSEPH STRESINO, of Forest Hills, N. Y. Writing. A Collection of Poems.

HELEN SHIRLEY THOMAS, of Baltimore, Md., A. B. Goucher College, 1953. Political Science.
United Nations' Work in the Field of Nationality: Practical Application and Theoretical Approach.

PETER EN-TIEN WEI, of Baltimore, Md., B. A. The Catholic University of America, 1953. Chemistry.

CECIL HILBURN WOMBLE, JR., of Birmingham, Ala., B. A. The Johns Hopkins University, 1954. Classics.

ROSALIND JUDITH ZUKOFF, of New York, N. Y., A. B. Hunter College, 1954. Romance Languages.

(48)

DOCTORS OF PHILOSOPHY

WITH TITLES OF DISSERTATIONS

JOHN GAGE ALLEE, JR., of Washington, D. C., B. A. George Washington University, 1939; A. M. 1940. English.
The Differentiated Plural in English.

CECIL RAVENSCROFT BALL, of College Park, Md., A. B. College of William and Mary, 1923; A. M. University of Maryland, 1934. English.
A Phonemic Analysis of Early West Saxon.

ARTHUR CHESTER BANKS, JR., of Baltimore, Md., B. S. St. John's University, 1939; M. A. New York University, 1945. Political Science.
International Law Governing Prisoners of War during the Second World War.

ROBERT WAUCHOPE BASS, of Annapolis, Md., B. A. The Johns Hopkins University, 1950, A. B. University of Oxford, 1952. Mathematics.
On the Singularities of Certain Non-linear Systems of Differential Equations.

RICHARD PAUL BENTON, of Baltimore, Md., B. S. The Johns Hopkins University 1952; M. A. 1953. Aesthetics of Literature.
The Aesthetics of Friedrich Nietzsche: The Relation of Art to Life.

STANLEY BLOCK, of Baltimore, Md., M. A. The Johns Hopkins University, 1952. Chemistry.
The Crystal Structure of $K_2V_6O_{16}$.

EMIL BORYSKO, of Brooklyn, N. Y., B. A. Brooklyn College, 1940; M. A. George Washington University, 1951. Biology.
An Evaluation, by Phase Contrast Microscopy, of the Methacrylate Embedding Technique Used in the Electron Microscopy of Cells.

STEPHEN DESIDERIUS BRUCK, of Baltimore, Md., B. S. Boston College, 1951; M. A. The Johns Hopkins University, 1953. Chemistry.
The Preparation and Some Properties of Imidazole Heme Complexes.

GEORGE CARROLL BUZBY, JR., of Baltimore, Md., A. B. Princeton University, 1950; M. A. The Johns Hopkins University, 1951. Chemistry.
Experiments in the Glutaconic Ester Series.

THOMAS ARTHUR CARLSON, of West Hartford, Conn., B. S. Trinity College, 1950; M. A. The Johns Hopkins University, 1951. Chemistry.
Studies in Hot Atom Chemistry.

PAUL ROBERT CHAGNON, of Woonsocket, R. I., B. S. College of the Holy Cross, 1950. Physics.
Neutron Angular Distributions.

CHE-TYAN CHANG, of Shanghai, China, B. A. Chiao Tung University, 1943; M. S. University of Illinois, 1950. Aeronautics.
On the Interaction of Weak Disturbances and a Plane Shock of Arbitrary Strength in a Perfect Gas.

BOA-TEH CHU, of Long Island, N. Y., B. S. National Central University, China, 1945. Aeronautics.
Some Contributions to the Theory of Combustion Aerodynamics.

RALPH KIRBY DAVIDSON, of Missoula, Mont., B. A. University of Oxford, 1951; M. A. The Johns Hopkins University, 1953. Political Economy.
Price Discrimination in Selling Gas and Electricity.

WILLIAM EDWARD DOSSEL, of Pine Bluff, Ark., A. B. Illinois College, 1948; M. S. Marquette University, 1950. Biology.
An Experimental Study of the Structural and Functional Development of the Thyroid of the Chick Embryo.

JAMES ANDREW ENGLISH, of Bethesda, Md., B. S. Pennsylvania State College, 1932; D. D. S. University of Pennsylvania, 1936; M. S. 1948. Biology.
A Biochemical and Histological Study of Radiated and Normal Salivary Glands.

JOHN MAJOR FOWLER, of Albany, Ga., B. S. Earlham College, 1949; M. S. University of Oklahoma, 1950. Physics.
The Be^9 (n, 2n) Be^8 Reaction.

COY MONTGOMERY GLASS, of Dayton, Ohio, B. E. The Johns Hopkins University, 1949; M. A. 1951. Mechanical Engineering.
A Method for Studying Metals at Elevated Temperatures Using X-Rays and an Application of this Method to Molybdenum.

MILTON ALLAN GOLDBERG, of Chicago, Ill., A. B. University of New Mexico, 1948; M. A. University of Chicago, 1949. English.
The Novels of Tobias Smollett: Analysis in an Eighteenth-Century Mode.

WILLARD HUNTINGTON GRANT, of West Hartford, Conn., A. B. Emory University, 1948. Geology.
The Geology of Hart County, Georgia.

SIMEON KAHN HENINGER, JR., of Monroe, La., B. S. Tulane University, 1944; B. A. 1947; M. A. 1949; B. Litt. University of Oxford, 1951. English.
A Study of Renaissance Meteorology in Relation to Elizabethan and Jacobean Literature.

PAUL HOROWICZ, of Baltimore, Md., B. A. New York University, 1951. Biophysics.
The Relation of Glycolysis to Function in Sympathetic and Somatic Nervous Tissue.

JOHN EDWARD HUESMAN, S. J., of San Francisco, Calif., A. B. Gonzaga University, 1942; M. A. 1943; S. T. L. Alma College, 1950. Oriental Seminary.
The Infinitive Absolute in Biblical Hebrew and Related Dialects.

HORACE DWIGHT HUMMEL, of Baltimore, Md., A. B. Concordia Seminary, 1947; M. S. T. 1952. Oriental Seminary.
Enclitic Mem in Early Northwest Semitic, with Special Reference to Hebrew.

VERNON JAMES HURST, of Atlanta, Ga., B. S. University of GEORGIA, 1951; M. S. Emory University, 1952. Geology.
The Stratigraphy and Structure of the Mineral Bluff Quadrangle.

JOHN ERIC IWERSEN, of Baltimore, Md., B. S. Wagner Memorial Lutheran College, 1949; A. M. The Johns Hopkins University, 1951. Chemistry.
The Study of Tritons as Bombarding Particles and The Measurement of Gamma Rays from Some Light Nuclei.

LUDWELL HARRISON JOHNSON, III, of Baltimore, Md., B. A. The Johns Hopkins University, 1952. History.
War, Politics, and Cotton: The Red River Expedition of 1864.

STANLEY KELLEY, JR., of Baltimore, Md., A. B. University of Kansas, 1949; M. A. 1951. Political Science.
The Role of the Public Relations Man in American Politics.

ALAN LEE KISTLER, of Baltimore, Md., B. E. The Johns Hopkins University, 1950; M. S. E. The Johns Hopkins University, 1952. Aeronautics.
I. Turbulence and Temperature Fluctuations behind a Heated Grid.
II. Relative Diffusion behind Two Line Sources in Homogeneous Turbulence.

ALBERT JOSEPH KUHN, of Arlington Heights, Ill, B. A. University of Illinois, 1950. English.
Concepts of Mythology and their Relations to English Literature: 1700-1830.

HOWARD MAER LENHOFF, of North Adams, Mass., A. B. Coe College, 1950. Biology.
Alternative Pathways of Terminal Electron Transfer in *Pseudomonas fluorescens*.

LIONEL JOHN LERNER, of Chicago, Ill., A. B. The University of Chicago, 1950; A. M., 1952. Political Economy.
Theories of Imperialist Exploitation.

PETER MICHAEL LEWINSOHN, of Baltimore, Md., B. S. Allegheny College, 1951; M. A. The Johns Hopkins University, 1953. Psychology.
Some Individual Differences in Physiological Reactivity to Stress.

ROBERT LISLE, of Ruxton, Md., A. B. Harvard College,

1950; M. A. The Johns Hopkins University, 1953. Classics.

The Cults of Corinth.

BRUCE CHARLES LUTZ, of Newark, Del., B. A. University of Western Ontario, 1942; M. A., 1944. Physics.

The Structure of Paradichlorobenzene as Determined by Nuclear Quadrupole Spectroscopy.

JOHN LESTER MELTON, of Baltimore, Md., B. A. University of Utah, 1948. English.

Aspects of Comedy in the English Chivalric Romances.

MICHAEL MICHAELY, of Jerusalem, Israel, A. M. The Hebrew University of Jerusalem, 1952. Political Economy.

Devaluation and Dual Markets under Inflation with Direct Controls.

KENNETH EUGENE MILLER, of Chapman, Kans., A. B. University of Kansas, 1949; A. M., 1951. Political Science.

The British Labour Party and Theories of Socialist Foreign Policy, 1900-1931.

JAMES GREGORY MOORE, of Palo Alto, Calif., B. S. Stanford University, 1951; M. S. University of Washington, 1952. Geology.

Geology of the Sierra Nevada Front near Mt. Baxter, California.

FRANK CHAPPELL OGG, JR., of Bowling Green, Ohio, B. A. Bowling Green State University, 1950; M. A. The Johns Hopkins University, 1955. Mathematics.

The Domain of Existence of the Isoperiodic Families of the First Kind in the Restricted Problem of Three Bodies.

RAYMOND EDWIN OLSON, of Baltimore, Md., A. B. Columbia University, 1950. Philosophy.

Hobbes's Logical Conventionalism.

DONALD JAMES PORTMAN, of Los Altos, Calif., B. S. University of Michigan, 1946. Geography.

An Investigation of the Theory and Measurement of Heat Transfer in Natural Soil.

ALFRED PROCK, of Baltimore, Md., B. E. The Johns Hopkins University, 1951; M. A. 1953. Chemistry.

Dielectric Studies of Amorphous Oxides.

GERRIT HUBBARD ROELOFS, of Dover, N. H., B. A. Amherst College, 1942. English.

The Law of Nature, the Tradition, and the Faerie Queene.

BENJAMIN TURNER SANKEY, JR., of Baltimore, Md., A. B. The Johns Hopkins University, 1951; A. M. 1951. Aesthetics of Literature.

The Romantic Satan: A Study in the Aesthetics of Literature.

RALPH ERNEST SEGEL, of Putnam Valley, N. Y., B. S. Massachusetts Institute of Technology, 1948. Physics.

Polarization of the Protons Produced in the Deuteron-Deuteron Reaction.

JOSEPH STERNBERG, of Aberdeen, Md., B. S. E. California Institute of Technology, 1942; M. S. 1943. Aeronautics.

The Transition from a Turbulent to a Laminar Boundary Layer.

PAUL WINDOM SUTTON, JR., of Cincinnati, Ohio, A. B. University of Cincinnati, 1950. Philosophy.

The Role of Fact in Moral Judgment.

LESLIE JAMES TODD, of Kent, Ohio, B. S. Kent State University, 1951; M. A. The Johns Hopkins University, 1953. Chemistry.

Automatic Calorimetry.

DAVID WILLIAM TREXLER, of Denver, Colo., B. S. Southern Methodist University, 1941, Geology.

Stratigraphy and Structure of the Coalville area, Northeastern Utah.

WILLIAM BENTLEY WALKER, of New Haven, Conn., A. B. Harvard College, 1944; M. A. The Johns Hopkins University, 1951. History of Medicine.

The Health Reform Movement in the United States 1830-1870.

ROBERT WINTHROP WATSON, of Greensboro, N. C., B. A. Williams College, 1946; M. A. The Johns Hopkins University, 1950. English.

The Novels of George Meredith.

KENNETH NEWCOMER WEAVER, of Lancaster, Pa., B. S. Franklin and Marshall College, 1950. Geology.

The Geology of the Hanover Area, York County, Pennsylvania.

ALBERT MALCOLM WITTENBERG, of Morristown, N. J., B. S. Union College, 1949. Physics.

The Zeeman Effect in the 3d Complexes of the Hydrogen Molecule.

JOHN BRUNO WOLFF, of Baltimore, Md., A. B. Hunter College, 1950; A. M. The Johns Hopkins University, 1951. Biology.

Studies on the Bacterial Metabolism of Hexitols.

H. LYNN WOMACK, of Washington, D. C., A. B. George Washington University, 1949. Philosophy.

The Mission of America (1815-1860), an Historical Study of an Idea.

HENRY JAMES YOUNG, of York, Pa., A. B. Franklin and Marshall College, 1932. History.

The Treatment of the Loyalists in Pennsylvania.

JOHN YOUNG, of Washington, D. C., B. A. Tokyo Imperial University, 1942; B. S. Georgetown University, 1949; M. S. 1951. History.

Japanese Historians and the Location of Yamadai.

(58)

CPSIA information can be obtained
at www.ICGtesting.com
Printed in the USA
BVHW041455150219
540385BV00008B/148/P